A
KNOCK KNOCK
JOKE A DAY

TWO SPECIAL GIFTS FOR OUR READERS

AS A SPECIAL THANK YOU FOR GETTING THIS BOOK, WE'D LIKE TO GIVE YOU:

A BOOK EXCLUSIVE (AVAILABLE ONLY WITH THIS BOOK)

THE SURPRISING PSYCHOLOGY OF LAUGHTER, AND 10 UNIQUE TOOLS & TECHNIQUES FOR YOU TO MAKE LAUGHTER AN EVERYDAY HABIT FOR THE FAMILY

+

A MONTH OF FRESH DAD JOKES

IF YOU LIKE KNOCK KNOCK JOKES, THEN HERE'S AN EXTRA 31 DAYS OF FRESH DAD JOKES TO USE ON YOUR UNSUSPECTING VICTIM!

New Message — ✕ ×

To: theluckyreader@message.com

Subject: Dad Joke of the Day!

WHY DID THE GOLFER CHANGE HIS PANTS?

BECAUSE HE GOT A HOLE IN ONE!

VISIT WWW.DADDILIFE.COM/LOL TO GET YOURS!

TABLE OF CONTENTS

INTRODUCTION

Knock-Knock
Who's there?
Dad.
Dad who?
Dad's a good knock-knock joke!

Welcome to the world of the Knock Knock joke. We won't leave you standing outside. Come on in!

Knock Knock jokes are loved the world over. It doesn't matter whether you're 5 or 95; they're always good fun. The repetitive format and silly wordplay make them perfect jokes to tell the family. They are perfect for dads to use. In essence, they fall under the "Dad Joke" category – a category that's part of every dad's right of passage. Knock Knock jokes elicit the outcome of a groan and an eye roll, and that's all part of the fun. Although for young kids they can be genuinely funny as they start to develop their sense of humor!

In this book, we'll give you a collection of 366 (yep, we've got leap years covered, too) of the best knock-knock jokes. But beyond that, we also look at the surprising history of the Knock Knock joke and get advice from the DaddiLife community on how best to deliver them.

WHO ARE DADDILIFE BOOKS, AND WHY THIS BOOK?

DaddiLife Books have put this collection of knock-knock jokes together.

DaddiLife is an online community of more than 150,000 dads from around the world sharing stories, advice, guides, and interviews that shine a light on what it means to be a modern-day dad.

Check us out at www.daddilife.com

We're a team of more than 50 writers who have been telling knock-knock jokes to all our kids since 2014 and have tested every single one of the 366 in this collection on our own real-live subjects, whether they signed up for it or not.

So without further ado, let's open the door and jump right in!

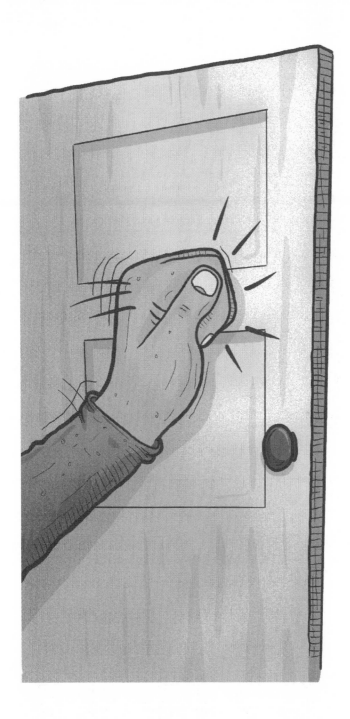

THE HISTORY OF THE KNOCK KNOCK

Knock-Knock
Who's there?
Keanu.
Keanu who?
**Keanu believe how much history there is
about the knock-knock joke?!**

by exhibiting a pseudo-intellectual activity. And since no one could possibly guess the right answer to these games, the person starting any of them has a feeling of superiority, a false belief that he is smarter than the other person."

Today Today knock-knock jokes are all the rage. Google them, and you'll find new ones are being added all the time.

In our research for this book, we were amazed at how many Knock Knock joke niches we found online. There are collections of knock-knock jokes for online dating: "Knock! Knock! Who's there? Dubai. Dubai who? Would you allow me Dubai you a drink?" There are Knock Knock jokes for actuarial statisticians: "Knock! Knock! Who's there? Em. Em who? MLE! The Maximum Likelihood Estimator!" (we suspect you need to be a statistician to understand that one). And there was this fun meme going around too that said:

"Whoever invented knock-knock jokes should get a no bell prize."

HOW TO DELIVER A KNOCK-KNOCK JOKE

Knock, knock!
Who's there?
Gus.
Gus who?
That's what you're supposed to do!

So much of joke-telling is about delivery. As the adage goes, "it's not only what you say but also how you say it." When it comes to telling jokes, we consulted the dads across the DaddiLife community.

The first thing to understand is what the Knock-Knock joke is intended to do. Here are the three golden objectives:

A. It's a form of Dad Joke; it's not meant to be clever.

B. The perfect reaction is a "urgh daaa-aad" groan.

C. You get a extra bonus if you get a little giggle at the end of the groan.

Now that you've got your objectives clear let's look at how to deliver them.

. . . .

01 Single out your victim.

"COMEDY VICTIM"

It's often good to start by singling out your victim with a "Hey [first name]!"

02 Don't ask, tell.

Once you have their attention, don't ask, "you wanna hear a knock-knock joke?" because you're probably going to get a "no." Just dive straight into it.

03 Everyone knows the rules.

One of the great things about a knock-knock joke is that everyone knows how to play along. Everyone knows to say, "who's there?" I don't know where we all learn this from, perhaps it's part of the universal human consciousness, but everyone knows the deal.

04 Bring out the drama

Although a knock-knock joke is short, it can still be heightened by a dramatic delivery. Here's how to do it:

- Say "knock-knock" with a serious and deadpan voice.
- After the "who's there," wait for two seconds before replying. That small pause sets up a little intrigue.
- After the "XYZ who?" reply immediately without pause.
- When you deliver your punchline, open your eyes wide and say it with a tone that starts low and builds up in pitch, so you end the punchline on a high note. This tells your victim that you're being silly and that you're expecting a groan.

With all the being said, the beauty of the knock-knock joke is that you simply cannot get it wrong. There's absolutely no need to feel anxious about it. Of all the joke formats in the world, the knock-knock joke is the easiest to get right. That's why it's so popular for kids, and that's why usually it's the first kind of joke we tell in our lives.

JANUARY

Knock, knock!
Who's there?
Phyllis.
Phyllis who?
Phyllis in on the news!

01

JANUARY

Knock, knock.
Who's there?
Goliath.
Goliath who?
Goliath down, you look-eth tired!

02

JANUARY

Knock, knock.
Who's there?
Wooden shoe.
Wooden shoe who?
Wooden shoe like to hear another joke?

03

JANUARY

Knock, knock.
Who's there?
Amish.
Amish who?
Really? You don't look like a shoe!

04
JANUARY

Knock, knock.
Who's there?
Boo.
Boo who?
Why are you crying?

05
JANUARY

Knock, knock.
Who's there?
A little old lady.
A little old lady who?
I didn't know you could yodel!

06
JANUARY

Knock, knock.
Who's there?
Harry.
Harry who?
Harry up and answer the door!

07
JANUARY

Knock, knock.
Who's there?
Cash.
Cash who?
No thanks, but I'll take a peanut if you have one!

08
JANUARY

Knock, knock.
Who's there?
Canoe.
Canoe who?
Canoe come out and play with me?

09
JANUARY

Knock, knock.
Who's there?
Lettuce.
Lettuce who?
Lettuce in, it's cold out here!

10
JANUARY

Knock, knock.
Who's there?
Mikey.
Mikey who?
Mikey doesn't fit in the keyhole!

11
JANUARY

Knock, knock.
Who's there?
Cows go.
Cows go who?
No silly, cows go MOO!

12
JANUARY

Knock, knock.
Who's there?
Stopwatch.
Stopwatch who?
Stopwatch you're doing and let me in!

13
JANUARY

Knock, knock.
Who's there?
I am.
I am who?
You don't know who you are?

14
JANUARY

Knock, knock.
Who's there?
Yah.
Yah who?
No, I prefer Google.

15
JANUARY

Knock, knock.
Who's there?
Nana.
Nana who?
Nana your business!

16

JANUARY

Knock, knock.
Who's there?
Justin.
Justin who?
Justin the neighborhood and thought I'd come over!

17

JANUARY

Knock, knock.
Who's there?
Theodore.
Theodore who?
Theodore is stuck and it won't open!

18

JANUARY

Knock, knock.
Who's there?
Nuisance.
Nuisance who?
What's new since yesterday?

19
JANUARY

Knock, knock.
Who's there?
Banana.
Banana who?
Knock, knock.
Who's there?
Banana.
Banana who?
(repeat a few more times)
Knock, knock.
Who's there?
Orange.
Orange who?
Orange you glad I didn't say banana?

20
JANUARY

Knock, knock.
Who's there?
Atch.
Atch who?
Bless you!

21
JANUARY

Knock, knock.
Who's there?
Spell.
Spell who?
Okay, w-h-o.

22
JANUARY

Knock, knock!
Who's there?
Stu.
Stu who?
Stu late to ask questions.

23
JANUARY

Knock, knock.
Who's there?
Tank.
Tank who?
You're welcome!

24
JANUARY

Knock, knock.
Who's there?
Cargo.
Cargo who?
No, car go BEEP BEEP!

25
JANUARY

Knock, knock.
Who's there?
Leaf.
Leaf who?
Leaf me alone!

26
JANUARY

Knock, knock.
Who's there?
Candice.
Candice who?
Candice door open, or what?

27

JANUARY

Knock, knock.
Who's there?
Isabel.
Isabel who?
Isabel working? I had to knock!

28

JANUARY

Knock, knock.
Who's there?
Dishes.
Dishes who?
Dishes me! How are you?

29

JANUARY

Knock Knock.
Who's there?
Europe.
Europe Who?
No, YOU'RE a poo!

30

JANUARY

Knock knock.
Who's there?
Honeydew.
Honeydew who?
Honeydew you wanna dance?

31
JANUARY

Knock knock.
Who's there?
Whoo.
Whoo who?
Thank you! Can I get some applause?

FEBRUARY

Knock Knock!
Who's there?
Barbara.
Barbara who?
**Barbara black sheep have
you any wool?**

1
FEBRUARY

Knock knock.
Who's there?
Ray D.
Ray D. who?
Ray D or not, here I come.

2
FEBRUARY

Knock knock.
Who's there?
Shore.
Shore who?
Shore hope you love these knock-knock jokes!

3
FEBRUARY

Knock, knock!
Who's there?
Shirley.
Shirley who?
Shirley I don't have to tell you!

34

4

FEBRUARY

Knock, knock!
Who's there?
Oscar.
Oscar who?
Oscar a silly question, get a silly answer!

5

FEBRUARY

Knock knock.
Who's there?
Oswald.
Oswald who?
Os-wal-d my bubble gum!

6

FEBRUARY

Knock knock.
Who's there?
Will.
Will who?
Will you open the door?

7
FEBRUARY

Knock knock.
Who's there?
Tatt.
Tatt who?
I'm too young for a tattoo. Maybe when I'm older.

8
FEBRUARY

Knock knock.
Who's there?
One.
One who?
One two three. Testing.

9
FEBRUARY

Knock, knock!
Who's there?
Carmen.
Carmen who?
Carmen get it. I have hot pizza!

10
FEBRUARY

Knock knock.
Who's there?
Beats.
Beats who?
Beats me.

11
FEBRUARY

Knock! Knock!
Who's there?
Déjà.
Déjà who?
Knock! Knock!

12
FEBRUARY

Knock! Knock!
Who's there?
A broken pencil.
A broken pencil who?
Never mind, it's pointless.

13
FEBRUARY

Knock! Knock!
Who's there?
Honeybee.
Honeybee who?
Honey bee a dear and open the door, please.

14
FEBRUARY

Knock! Knock!
Who's there?
Olive.
Olive who?
And I love you too!

15
FEBRUARY

Knock! Knock!
Who's there?
Robin.
Robin who?
Robin you — hand over the cash!

16
FEBRUARY

Knock! Knock!
Who's there?
Two knee.
Two knee who?
Two knee fish!

17
FEBRUARY

Knock! Knock!
Who's there?
Nose.
Nose who?
I nose plenty more knock-knock jokes!

18
FEBRUARY

Knock! Knock!
Who's there?
Howl.
Howl who?
How'l you know if you don't open the door?

19

FEBRUARY

Knock! Knock!
Who's there?
A herd.
A herd who?
A herd you were home, so I came over!

20

FEBRUARY

Knock! Knock!
Who's there?
Urine.
Urine who?
Urine trouble if you don't answer the door.

21

FEBRUARY

Knock! Knock!
Who's there?
Voodoo.
Voodoo who?
Voodoo you think you are!?

22
FEBRUARY

Knock! Knock!
Who's there?
Dwayne.
Dwayne who?
Dwayne the bathtub already. I'm drowning!

23
FEBRUARY

Knock! Knock!
Who's there?
A pile up.
A pile up who?
Ewwww!

24
FEBRUARY

Knock! Knock!
Who's there?
Closure.
Closure who?
Closure mouth while you're chewing!

25
FEBRUARY

Knock! Knock!
Who's there?
Says.
Says who?
Says me, that's who!

26
FEBRUARY

Knock, knock!
Who's there?
Luke.
Luke who?
Luke through the peephole and find out.

27
FEBRUARY

Knock, knock.
Who's there?
Figs.
Figs who?
Figs the doorbell, it's not working!

28

FEBRUARY

Knock, knock.
Who's there?
Hal.
Hal who?
Hal will you know if you don't open the door?

29

FEBRUARY

Knock, knock.
Who's there?
Annie.
Annie who?
Annie thing you can do, I can do too!

MARCH

Knock, knock!
Who's there?
Sadie.
Sadie who?
Sadie magic word and watch me disappear!

1

MARCH

Knock! Knock!
Who's There?
Oink Oink.
Oink Oink who?
Make up your mind. Are you a pig or an owl?

2

MARCH

Knock knock.
Who's there?
Noah.
Noah who?
No-a-nyone who can open this door?

3

MARCH

Knock, knock.
Who's there?
Interrupting Dog.
Interrupting – d- ?
WOOF WOOF WOOF (interrupt them early!)

4
MARCH

Knock, knock.
Who's there?
To.
To who?
It's to whom.

5
MARCH

Knock, knock.
Who's there?
Snow.
Snow who?
Snow use. The joke is over.

6
MARCH

Knock, knock.
Who's there?
Hawaii.
Hawaii who?
I'm good. Hawaii you?

7

MARCH

Knock, knock.
Who's there?
Woo.
Woo who?
Glad you're excited, too!

8

MARCH

Knock, knock.
Who's there?
Anita.
Anita who?
Let me in! Anita borrow something.

9

MARCH

Knock, knock.
Who's there?
Water.
Water who?
Water you doing telling jokes right now?
Don't you have other things to do?

10

MARCH

Knock, knock.
Who's there?
Leaf.
Leaf who?
Leaf me alone!

11
MARCH

Knock, knock.
Who's there?
Needle.
Needle who?
Needle little help right now!

12
MARCH

Knock, knock.
Who's there?
Amos.
Amos who?
A mosquito. Look, right there!

13
MARCH

Knock, knock.
Who's there?
Thermos.
Thermos who?
Ther-mos be a better way to get to you.

50

14
MARCH

Knock, knock.
Who's there?
Razor.
Razor who?
Razor hands, this is a stick-up!

15
MARCH

Knock, knock.
Who's there?
Amarillo.
Amarillo who?
Amarillo nice person.

16
MARCH

Knock, knock.
Who's there?
Cher.
Cher who?
Cher would be nice if you opened the door!

17
MARCH

Knock, knock.
Who's there?
Icy.
Icy who?
Icy you looking at me!

18
MARCH

Knock, knock.
Who's there?
Mustache.
Mustache who?
I mustache you a question.

19
MARCH

Knock, knock.
Who's there?
Alex.
Alex who?
Alex-plain later!

20
MARCH

Knock, knock.
Who's there?
Iva.
Iva who?
I've a sore hand from knocking!

21
MARCH

Knock, knock.
Who's there?
Watson.
Watson who?
Watson TV right now?

22
MARCH

Knock, knock.
Who's there?
Anee.
Anee who?
Anee one you like!

53

23
MARCH

Knock, knock.
Who's there?
Althea.
Althea who?
Althea later alligator!

24
MARCH

Knock, knock.
Who's there?
Arfur.
Arfur who?
Ar-fur got!

25
MARCH

Knock, Knock!
Who's there?
Radio.
Radio who?
Radio not, here I come!

26
MARCH

Knock, knock.
Who's there?
Yukon.
Yukon who?
Yu-kon say that again!

27
MARCH

Knock, knock.
Who's there?
Viper.
Viper who?
Viper nose, it's running!

28
MARCH

Knock, knock.
Who's there?
CD.
CD who?
CD person on your doorstep?

29
MARCH

Knock! Knock!
Who's there?
Two knee.
Two knee who?
Two knee your piano, and it'll sound better.

30
MARCH

Knock, knock.
Who's there?
Claire.
Claire who?
Claire a path, I'm coming through!

31
MARCH

Knock knock.
Who's there?
Roach.
Roach who?
Roach you a message. Did you get it?

APRIL

Knock, knock!
Who's there?
Candy.
Candy who?
Candy Easter Bunny carry all those treats in one basket?

1
APRIL

Knock, knock!
Who's there?
Haven.
Haven who?
Haven you heard enough of these knock-knock jokes?

2
APRIL

Knock, knock!
Who's there?
Avenue.
Avenue who?
Avenue knocked on this door before?

3
APRIL

Knock, knock!
Who's there?
Justin.
Justin who?
Justin time for dinner.

4
APRIL

Knock, knock!
Who's there?
Ben.
Ben who?
Ben knocking for 10 minutes!

5
APRIL

Knock, knock!
Who's there?
Alien.
Alien who?
Um, how many aliens do you know?

6
APRIL

Knock, knock!
Who's there?
Andrew.
Andrew who?
An-drew a picture!

7

APRIL

Knock, knock!
Who's there?
Armageddon.
Armageddon who?
Armageddon a little bored. Let's go out.

8

APRIL

Knock, knock!
Who's there?
Leon.
Leon who?
Leon me when you're not strong!

9

APRIL

Knock, knock!
Who's there?
Wa Wa.
Wa Wa who?
What are you so excited about?!

10
APRIL

Knock, knock!
Who's there?
I am.
I am who?
Don't you even know who you are?!

11
APRIL

Knock, knock!
Who's there?
Ratio.
Ratio who?
Ratio to the end of the street!

12
APRIL

Knock, knock!
Who's there?
Ice cream soda.
Ice cream soda who?
Ice scream soda people can hear me!

13
APRIL

Knock, knock!
Who's there?
Impatient Pirate.
Impatient P- ?
ARRRRRR! (interrupt them early!)

14
APRIL

Knock, knock!
Who's there?
Keith.
Keith who?
Keith me, right now

15
APRIL

Knock, knock!
Who's there?
June.
June who?
June know how long I've been knocking out here?

16
APRIL

Knock, knock!
Who's there?
Dejav.
Dejav who?
Knock, knock

17
APRIL

Knock, knock!
Who's there?
Passion.
Passion who?
Passion through and thought I'd say hello.

18
APRIL

Knock, knock!
Who's there?
Kenya.
Kenya who?
Kennnnnya feel the love tonight?

19
APRIL

Knock, knock!
Who's there?
Opportunity.
Opportunity who?
Opportunity waits for no one.

20
APRIL

Knock, knock!
Who's there?
Champ.
Champ who?
Champ poo your hair – it's dirty!

21
APRIL

Knock, knock!
Who's there?
Howard.
Howard who?
Howard I know?

22
APRIL

Knock, knock!
Who's there?
Odysseus.
Odysseus who?
Odysseus the last straw!

23
APRIL

Knock, knock!
Who's there?
Icing.
Icing who?
Icing so loudly so everyone can hear me!

24
APRIL

Knock, knock!
Who's there?
Sara!
Sara who?
Sara 'nother way in?

25
APRIL

Knock, knock!
Who's there?
Sweden.
Sweden who?
Sweden sour chicken, please!

26
APRIL

Knock, knock!
Who's there?
Pecan.
Pecan who?
Pecan someone your own size.

27
APRIL

Knock, knock!
Who's there?
Weirdo.
Weirdo who?
Weirdo you think you're going?

28
APRIL

Knock, Knock!
Who's there?
Wooden shoe.
Wooden shoe who?
Wooden shoe like to hear more jokes?

29
APRIL

Knock knock.
Who's there?
Omelette.
Omelette who?
Omelette you finish.

30
APRIL

Knock knock.
Who's there?
You.
You who?
You hoo, anybody home?

69

MAY

Knock, knock!
Who's there?
Gorilla.
Gorilla who?
Gorilla me a hamburger!

1
MAY

Knock, knock.
Who's there?
Norma Lee.
Norma Lee who?
**Norma Lee I don't knock on random doors,
but I had to meet you!**

2
MAY

Knock, knock.
Who's there?
Adore.
Adore who?
Adore is between us, so open it!

3
MAY

Knock, knock!
Who's there?
A Mayan.
A Mayan who?
A Mayan in the way?

4
MAY

Knock, knock!
Who's there?
Maida.
Maida who?
Maida force be with you!

5
MAY

Knock knock.
Who's there?
Rhonda.
Rhonda who?
Rendezvous here at 2300. Knock twice.

73

6
MAY

Knock knock.
Who's there?
Turnip.
Turnip who?
Turnip the volume, I love this song!

7
MAY

Knock knock.
Who's there?
Taco.
Taco who?
Taco to you later. It's taking too long for you to open the door.

8
MAY

Knock knock.
Who's there?
Tyrone.
Tyrone who?
Tyrone shoelaces!

9
MAY

Knock knock.
Who's there?
Yacht.
Yacht who?
Yacht to know me by now!

10
MAY

Knock knock.
Who's there?
Dishes.
Dishes who?
Dishes a nice place you got here.

11
MAY

Knock knock.
Who's there?
Rhino!
Rhino who?
Rhino every knock-knock joke there is!

12
MAY

Knock knock.
Who's there?
Leena.
Leena who?
Leena little closer and I will tell you!

13
MAY

Knock knock.
Who's there?
Juno.
Juno who?
Juno I love you, right? (Try a Spanish accent for this one)

14
MAY

Knock, knock!
Who's there?
Frank.
Frank who?
Frank you for being my friend.

15
MAY

Knock, Knock!
Who's there?
Kanga.
Kanga who?
Actually it's Kangaroo.

16
MAY

Knock knock.
Who's there?
Egg.
Egg who?
Eggstremely disappointed you still don't recognize me.

17
MAY

Knock knock.
Who's there?
Zoom.
Zoom who?
Zoom did you expect!

18
MAY

Knock knock.
Who's there?
Ben.
Ben who?
Ben hoping I can come in!

19
MAY

Knock! Knock!
Who's there?
Want.
Want who?
Want, who ... three, four, five!

20
MAY

Knock knock.
Who's there?
Cook.
Cook who?
Yeah, you do sound cuckoo!

21
MAY

Knock knock.
Who's there?
Butter.
Butter who?
Butter be quick, I have to go to the bathroom!

22
MAY

Knock knock.
Who's there?
Ears.
Ears who?
Ears another knock-knock joke for you!

23
MAY

Knock knock.
Who's there?
Ferdie!
Ferdie who?
Ferdie last time, open dis door!

24
MAY

Knock Knock!
Who's there?
Andy.
Andy who?
And he bit me again.

25
MAY

Knock Knock!
Who's there?
Abe Lincoln.
Abe Lincoln who?
Aww, come on! Don't you know who Abe Lincoln is?

26
MAY

Knock Knock!
Who's there?
Warrior.
Warrior who?
Warrior been all my life?

27
MAY

Knock Knock!
Who's there?
Anita.
Anita who?
Anita nother minute to think it over.

28
MAY

Knock Knock!
Who's there?
Lego.
Lego who?
Lego of me and I'll tell you!

29
MAY

Knock, Knock!
Who's there?
Mustache.
Mustache who?
I mustache you a question, but I'll shave it for later!

30
MAY

Knock Knock!
Who's there?
Howard.
Howard who?
Howard you like a big kiss?

31
MAY

Knock Knock
Who's there?
Barbie.
Barbie who?
Barbie Q chicken.

JUNE

Knock knock.
Who's there?
Roach.
Roach who?
Roach you an email! When are you gonna reply?

1
JUNE

Knock knock.
Who's there?
Juno.
Juno who?
Juno how funny this is?

2
JUNE

Knock, knock.
Who's there?
Alfie.
Alfie who?
Alfie terrible if you don't let me in!

3
JUNE

Knock knock.
Who's there?
Sherlock.
Sherlock who?
Sherlock your door tight.

4
JUNE

Knock knock.
Who's there?
Zany.
Zany who?
Zany body home?

5
JUNE

Knock knock.
Who's there?
Noise.
Noise who?
Noise to see you!

6
JUNE

Knock Knock!
Who's there?
Nuisance.
Nuisance who?
What's nui-sance yesterday?

7

JUNE

Knock Knock!
Who's there?
Dwight.
Dwight who?
D'wight way is better than the wrong way.

8

JUNE

Knock Knock!
Who's there?
Foster.
Foster who?
Foster than a speeding bullet!

9

JUNE

Knock Knock!
Who's there?
Chicken.
Chicken who?
Chicken your pockets if you can't find your keys

10
JUNE

Knock! Knock!
Who's There?
Oink Oink.
Oink Oink who?
Make up your mind. Are you a pig or an owl?

11
JUNE

Knock! Knock!
Who's there?
No one.
No one who?
Remains silent

12
JUNE

Knock knock.
Who's there?
Through.
Through who?
Through the door, once you open it up.

13
JUNE

Knock! Knock!
Who's there?
Wendy.
Wendy who?
Wendy bell works again I won't have to knock anymore.

14
JUNE

Knock, knock!
Who's there?
Ahmed.
Ahmed who?
Ahmed a mistake, wrong house!

15
JUNE

Knock, knock!
Who's there?
Henriette.
Henriette who?
Henri etta worm that was in his apple!

16
JUNE

Knock, knock!
Who's there?
Rita.
Rita who?
Rita book, you might learn something!

17
JUNE

Knock, knock!
Who's there?
Schnauzer.
Schnauzer who?
Schnauzer day going?

18
JUNE

Knock, knock!
Who's there?
Sty.
Sty who?
Sty away from strangers!

19
JUNE

Knock, knock!
Who's there?
Tamara.
Tamara who?
Tamara is another day.

20
JUNE

Knock, knock!
Who's there?
Warner.
Warner who?
Warner lift to school?

21
JUNE

Knock, knock!
Who's there?
Whitcomb.
Whitcomb who?
Whitcomb first, the chicken or the egg?

22
JUNE

Knock, knock!
Who's there?
Giraffe.
Giraffe who?
Giraffe anything to eat? I'm starving!

23
JUNE

Knock, knock!
Who's there?
Moose.
Moose who?
Moose you be so nosy?

24
JUNE

Knock, knock!
Who's there?
Abyssinia.
Abyssinia who?
Abys-sinia around!

25
JUNE

Knock, knock!
Who's there?
Calder.
Calder who?
Calder police - I've been robbed!

26
JUNE

Knock, knock!
Who's there?
Phillip.
Phillip who?
Phillip the bag with money, this is a stick-up.

27
JUNE

Knock, knock!
Who's There?
Soup.
Soup who?
Souperman!

28
JUNE

Knock, knock!
Who's there?
Tick.
Tick who?
Tick 'em up and give me all your money!

29
JUNE

Knock, knock!
Who's there?
Ammonia.
Ammonia who?
Ammonia little kid!

30
JUNE

Knock, knock!
Who's there?
India.
India who?
India night time I go to sleep!

JULY

Knock Knock!
Who's there?
T-Rex.
T-Rex who?
**There's a T-Rex at your door and
you want to know his name!?!**

1
JULY

Knock, knock!
Who's there?
Brad.
Brad who?
I've got Brad news I'm afraid.

2
JULY

Knock knock.
Who's there?
Bed.
Bed who?
Bed you can't guess who I am!

3
JULY

Knock knock.
Who's there?
Lion.
Lion who?
Lion on your doorstep, open up!

4
JULY

Knock Knock!
Who's there?
Amos.
Amos who?
A mosquito bit me!

5
JULY

Knock Knock!
Who's there?
Yetta.
Yetta who?
Yetta nother mosquito!

6
JULY

Knock Knock!
Who's there?
Juicy.
Juicy who?
Jui-cy what I see?!

7
JULY

Knock, knock!
Who's there?
Goat.
Goat who?
Goat to the door and find out.

8
JULY

Knock, knock!
Who's there?
Senior.
Senior who?
Senior so nosy, I'm not going to tell you.

9
JULY

Knock, knock!
Who's there?
Sam.
Sam who?
Sam day you'll recognize me.

10
JULY

Knock, knock!
Who's there?
Susan.
Susan who?
Susan socks go on your feet!

11
JULY

Knock, knock!
Who's there?
Chimney.
Chimney who?
Chimney cricket! Have you seen Pinocchio?

12
JULY

Knock, knock!
Who's there?
Deduct.
Deduct who?
Donald Deduct.

13
JULY

Knock, knock!
Who's there?
Weevil.
Weevil who?
Weevil, weevil ROCK YOU!

14
JULY

Knock, knock!
Who's there?
Bean.
Bean who?
Bean a while since I last saw ya!

15
JULY

Knock, knock!
Who's there?
Bison.
Bison who?
Bison cookies? I'm a scout.

16
JULY

Knock knock.
Who's there?
Matt.
Matt who?
That's my full name, but my friends call me Matt.

17
JULY

Knock, knock!
Who's there?
Hammond.
Hammond who?
Hammond eggs for breakfast please!

18
JULY

Knock, knock.
Who's there?
Ice cream.
Ice cream who?
Ice cream if you don't let me in!

19
JULY

Knock, knock!
Who's there?
Nacho.
Nacho who?
Nacho business!

20
JULY

Knock, knock!
Who's there?
Europe.
Europe who?
Europe to no good!

21
JULY

Knock, knock!
Who's there?
Tibet.
Tibet who?
Early Tibet and early to rise!

22
JULY

Knock, knock!
Who's there?
Donch.
Donch who?
Donch you wanna open the door?

23
JULY

Knock, knock!
Who's there?
Eiffel.
Eiffel who?
Eiffel sick!

24
JULY

Knock, knock!
Who's there?
Dime.
Dime who?
Dime to tell another knock-knock joke.

25
JULY

Knock, knock!
Who's there?
Major.
Major who?
Major day with this joke, haven't I?

26
JULY

Knock, knock!
Who's there?
Hugh.
Hugh who?
Hugh is going to let me in then?

27
JULY

Knock, knock!
Who's there?
Allied.
Allied who?
Allied, you'll never know who this is!

106

28
JULY

Knock, knock!
Who's there?
Halibut.
Halibut who?
Hali-but lending me five dollars?

29
JULY

Knock, knock!
Who's there?
Toucan.
Toucan who?
Toucan play this game!

30

JULY

Knock, knock!
Who's there?
De Niro.
De Niro who?
De Niro I get to you, the happier I am!

31
JULY

Knock, knock.

Who's there?

Orange.

Orange who?

Orange you going to open the door?

AUGUST

Knock, knock.
Who's there?
Alpaca.
Alpaca who?
Alpaca the suitcase, you load the car!

1

AUGUST

Knock, knock.
Who's there?
Amanda.
Amanda who?
A man da fix your door!

2

AUGUST

Knock, knock!
Who's there?
Warren.
Warren who?
Warren you gonna open the door?

3

AUGUST

Knock, knock!
Who's there?
Some bunny.
Some bunny who?
Some bunny has been eating all my carrots!

4
AUGUST

Knock, knock.
Who's there?
Owls say.
Owls say who?
Yes, they do!

5
AUGUST

Knock, knock!
Who's there?
Geno.
Geno who?
Ge-no I can't remember my surname?

6
AUGUST

Knock, knock!
Who's there?
Les.
Les who?
Les go out for a picnic.

7
AUGUST

Knock, knock!
Who's there?
Theresa.
Theresa who?
There's a fly in my soup!

8
AUGUST

Knock, knock!
Who's there?
Wendy.
Wendy who?
Wendy time is right I'll tell you!

9
AUGUST

Knock, knock!
Who's there?
Eddy.
Eddy who?
Eddy idea how I can get in?

10
AUGUST

Knock, knock!
Who's there?
Harmony.
Harmony who?
Harmony knock-knock jokes do you expect me to know?

11
AUGUST

Knock, knock!
Who's there?
Gillette.
Gillette who?
If Gillette me in, I won't knock anymore.

12
AUGUST

Knock, knock!
Who's there?
Kyle.
Kyle who?
Kyle be good if you let me in!

13
AUGUST

Knock, knock!
Who's there?
Yoda.
Yoda who?
Yoda one who wanted to hear a knock knock joke.

14
AUGUST

Knock, knock!
Who's there?
Brittney Spears.
Brittney Spears who?
Knock, knock!
Who's there?
Oops! I did it again!

15
AUGUST

Knock, knock!
Who's there?
Cheese.
Cheese who?
For cheese a jolly good fellow!

16
AUGUST

Knock, knock!
Who's there?
Jamaica.
Jamaica who?
Jamaica great door opener!

17
AUGUST

Knock, knock!
Who's there?
Nadia.
Nadia who?
Nadia head while the music plays!

18
AUGUST

Knock, knock!
Who's there?
Alba.
Alba who?
Alba waiting here until you open this door!

19
AUGUST

Knock, knock!
Who's there?
Wicked.
Wicked who?
Wicked talk more if you let me in.

20
AUGUST

Knock, knock!
Who's there?
Adolf.
Adolf who?
Adolf ball hit me in the mouth!

21
AUGUST

Knock, knock!
Who's there?
Beezer.
Beezer who?
Beezer good at making honey.

22
AUGUST

Knock, knock!
Who's there?
Aladdin.
Aladdin who?
Aladdin the street wants a word with you!

23
AUGUST

Knock, knock!
Who's there?
Albert.
Albert who!
Albert you can't guess who this is!

24
AUGUST

Knock, knock!
Who's there?
Amarillo.
Amarillo who?
Amarillo nice guy!

25
AUGUST

Knock, knock!
Who's there?
Amigo.
Amigo who?
Amigo to bed now I'm tired.

26
AUGUST

Knock knock.
Who's there?
Ruff ruff.
Ruff ruff who?
Who let the dogs out? I heard barking!

27
AUGUST

Knock, knock!
Who's there?
Amy.
Amy who?
Amy fraid I've forgotten!

28
AUGUST

Knock, knock!
Who's there?
Utah.
Utah who?
Utah-king to me!

29
AUGUST

Knock, knock!
Who's there?
Claire.
Claire who?
Claire your throat before you speak!

30
AUGUST

Knock, knock!
Who's there?
Sloane.
Sloane who?
Sloanely outside. Let me in!

31
AUGUST

Knock, knock!
Who's there?
Heidi.
Heidi who?
Heidi 'cided to come over to play!

SEPTEMBER

Knock knock.
Who's there?
Bacon.
Bacon who?
Baking some cookies in there?
Smells delicious!

1

SEPTEMBER

Knock, knock!
Who's there?
Yvette.
Yvette who?
Yvette helps a lot of animals!

2

SEPTEMBER

Knock, knock!
Who's there?
Quacker!
Quacker who?
Quacker another bad joke and I'm leaving!

3

SEPTEMBER

Knock, knock!
Who's there?
Kenny.
Kenny who?
Kenny let me in!

126

4
SEPTEMBER

Knock, knock!
Who's there?
Hanover.
Hanover who?
Hanover your money!

5
SEPTEMBER

Knock, knock!
Who's there?
Anny.
Anny who?
Anny one you like!

6
SEPTEMBER

Knock, knock!
Who's there?
Beth.
Beth who?
Beth you can guess.

7

SEPTEMBER

Knock, knock!
Who's there?
Carl.
Carl who?
Carl get you there quicker than if you walk!

8

SEPTEMBER

Knock, knock!
Who's there?
Elsie.
Elsie who?
El-sie you around!

9

SEPTEMBER

Knock! Knock!
Who's there?
Abby.
Abby who?
Abby birthday to you!

10

SEPTEMBER

Knock, knock!
Who's there?
Hiram.
Hiram who?
Hiram fine, how are you?

11

SEPTEMBER

Knock, knock!
Who's there?
Ivor.
Ivor who?
Ivor message for you.

12

SEPTEMBER

Knock, knock!
Who's there?
Jester.
Jester who?
Jester minute. I'm still thinking.

13
SEPTEMBER

Knock, knock!
Who's there?
Joan.
Joan who?
Joan you remember me?

14
SEPTEMBER

Knock, knock!
Who's there?
Adair.
Adair who?
Ad air once but now I'm bald.

15
SEPTEMBER

Knock, knock!
Who's there?
Hugo.
Hugo who?
Hugo first!

16

SEPTEMBER

Knock, knock!

Who's there?

Beef.

Beef who?

Before I get cold, you'd better let me in!

17

SEPTEMBER

Knock, knock!

Who's there?

Gargoyle.

Gargoyle who?

If you Gargoyle with saltwater, your throat will feel better!

18
SEPTEMBER

Knock, knock!
Who's there?
Amsterdam
Amsterdam who?
Amster-dam tired of these corny knock knock jokes.

19
SEPTEMBER

Knock, knock!
Who's there?
Otto.
Otto who?
Otto know. I've got amnesia.

20
SEPTEMBER

Knock, knock!
Who's there?
Ike.
Ike who?
Ike-ant stop telling these jokes!

21

SEPTEMBER

Knock, knock!
Who's there?"
Knock. Knock
who?
Knock, Knock!

22

SEPTEMBER

Knock, knock!
Who's there?
Leonie.
Leonie who?
Leonie one who laughs at my knock knock jokes is you.

23

SEPTEMBER

Knock, knock!
Who's there?
Needle.
Needle who?
Needle little money if you don't mind!

24

SEPTEMBER

Knock, knock!
Who's there?
Maya.
Maya who?
Mayabilities are too great for such stupid jokes.

25

SEPTEMBER

Knock, knock!
Who's there?
Scott.
Scott who?
Scott to be funnier jokes than this.

26

SEPTEMBER

Knock, knock!
Who's there?
Tail.
Tail who?
Tail all your friends this joke.

27

SEPTEMBER

Knock, knock!
Who's there?
Argue.
Argue who?
Argue going to let me in or not!

28

SEPTEMBER

Knock, knock!
Who's there?
Fang.
Fang who?
Fangs for letting me in!

29

SEPTEMBER

Knock, knock!
Who's there?
Ivor.
Ivor who?
Ivor you let me in or I`ll climb through the window.

30

SEPTEMBER

Knock, knock!
Who's there?
Sherwood.
Sherwood who?
Sherwood like to come in!

OCTOBER

Knock knock.
Who's there?
Witches.
Witches who?
Witches the way to the store?

1

OCTOBER

Knock, knock!
Who's there?
Vidal.
Vidal who?
Vidal like for you to open this door!

2

OCTOBER

Knock, knock!
Who's there?
Yolanda.
Yolanda who?
Yolanda me some money?

3

OCTOBER

Knock, knock!
Who's there?
Hugh.
Hugh who?
Hugh've got to be kidding!

140

4

OCTOBER

Knock, knock!
Who's there?
Joshua.
Joshua who?
Joshua wait until I think of the answer.

5

OCTOBER

Knock, knock!
Who's there?
Lionel.
Lionel who?
Lion-el roar if you don't feed him!

6

OCTOBER

Knock, knock!
Who's there?
Dewey.
Dewey who?
Dewey have to do these jokes all night?

7

OCTOBER

Knock, knock!
Who's there?
Luke.
Luke who?
Luke like you want to hear another knock knock joke!

8

OCTOBER

Knock, knock!
Who's there?
Ken.
Ken who?
Ken I come in?

9

OCTOBER

Knock, knock!
Who's there?
Ivory.
Ivory who?
Ivory strong like Superman!

10

OCTOBER

Knock, knock!
Who's there?
Imogen.
Imogen who?
Imogen how nice it would be to open the door!

11

OCTOBER

Knock, knock!
Who's there?
Russian.
Russian who?
Stop Russian Me!

12

OCTOBER

Knock, knock!
Who's there?
Colleen.
Colleen who?
Colleen up this mess!

143

13
OCTOBER

Knock, knock!
Who's there?
Sodom.
Sodom who?
Sodom earlier, but didn't talk to them.

14
OCTOBER

Knock, knock!
Who's there?
Sid.
Sid who?
Sid down. It's time to eat!

15
OCTOBER

Knock, knock!
Who's there?
Lenny!
Lenny who?
Lenny in, I'm hungry!

16
OCTOBER

Knock knock.
Who's there?
Wood.
Wood who?
Would you care for another knock-knock joke?

17
OCTOBER

Knock, knock!
Who's there?
Owen.
Owen who?
O-wen are you going to let me in?

18
OCTOBER

Knock, knock!
Who's there?
Iowa.
Iowa who?
Iowa you a dollar!

19
OCTOBER

Knock, knock!
Who's there?
Wheelbarrow.
Wheelbarrow who?
Wheelbarrow some money and go on holiday!

20
OCTOBER

Knock, knock!
Who's there?
Jamal.
Jamal who?
Jamal shook up, stop yelling at me!

21

OCTOBER

Knock, knock!
Who's there?
Mary Lee.
Mary Lee who?
Mary Lee, Mary Lee, Mary Lee, Mary Lee, life is but a dream. Row row row your boat....

22

OCTOBER

Knock, knock!
Who's there?
Alex.
Alex who?
Hey, Alex the questions around here!

23

OCTOBER

Knock, knock!
Who's there?
Allison.
Allison who?
Al-lison against the door and I hear you were home!

24

OCTOBER

Knock, knock!
Who's there?
Dawn.
Dawn who?
Dawn leave me out in the cold!

25

OCTOBER

Knock, knock!
Who's there?
Ann.
Ann who?
An old friend!

26
OCTOBER

Knock, knock!
Who's there?
Barry.
Barry who?
Barry the treasure so no one will find it!

27
OCTOBER

Knock, knock!
Who's there?
Betty.
Betty who?
Betty ya don't know who this is!

28
OCTOBER

Knock, knock!
Who's there?
Caesar.
Caesar who?
Caesar quickly before she gets away!

29

OCTOBER

Knock, knock!
Who's there?
Chester.
Chester who?
Chester minute, Don't you recognize me?

30

OCTOBER

Knock, knock!
Who's there?
Oliver,
Oliver who?
Oliver troubles will soon be over.

31

OCTOBER

Knock, knock!
Who's there?
Danielle.
Danielle who?
Danielle at me, I heard you the first time.

NOVEMBER

Knock, knock!
Who's there?
Arthur.
Arthur who?
Arthur any Thanksgiving leftovers?

1

NOVEMBER

Knock, knock.
Who's there?
Freeze.
Freeze who?
Freeze a Jolly Good Fellow! Freeze a Jolly Good Fellow!
Freeze a Jolly Good Fellow! Which nobody can deny!

2

NOVEMBER

Knock, knock!
Who's there?
Handsome.
Handsome who?
Hand-some pizza to me please!

3

NOVEMBER

Knock, knock!
Who's there?
Plato.
Plato who?
Plat-o fish and chips please.

4

NOVEMBER

Knock, knock!
Who's there?
Nose!
Nose who?
I nose plenty more knock knock jokes, don't worry!

5

NOVEMBER

Knock, knock!
Who's there?
Emma.
Emma who?
Emma bit cold out here, can you let me in?

155

6

NOVEMBER

Knock, knock!
Who's there?
Howard.
Howard who?
Howard you like to stand out here in the cold while someone keeps saying "Who's there?"

7

NOVEMBER

Knock, knock!
Who's there?
Churchill.
Churchill who?
Church'ill be held on Sunday!

8
NOVEMBER

Knock, knock!
Who's there?
Lisa.
Lisa who?
Lisa you can do is let me in! (Try an Italian accent for this one)

9
NOVEMBER

Knock, knock!
Who's there?
Doorbell repairman!.
Doorbell repairman who?
Ding dong! My work here is done!

10
NOVEMBER

Knock, knock!
Who's there?
Gideon.
Gideon who?
Gideon your horse and let's go!

11
NOVEMBER

Knock, knock!
Who's there?
Gwen.
Gwen who?
Gwen will I see you again?

12
NOVEMBER

Knock, knock!
Who's there?
Jenny.
Jenny who?
Jenny'd to open the door right now!

13
NOVEMBER

Knock, knock!
Who's there?
Heaven.
Heaven who?
**Heaven you heard enough of these silly
Knock Knock jokes?**

14
NOVEMBER

Knock, knock!
Who's there?
Icon.
Icon who?
**Icon tell you another knock knock joke. Do you
want me to?**

15
NOVEMBER

Knock, knock!
Who's there?
Apple.
Apple who?
Apple your hair if you don't let me in!

16
NOVEMBER

Knock, knock!
Who's there?
Sing.
Sing who?
Whooo-oo-oo!

17
NOVEMBER

Knock, knock!
Who's there?
Ada.
Ada who?
You're Ada your mind!

18
NOVEMBER

Knock, knock!
Who's there?
Alvin.
Alvin who!
Alvin a great time, how about you?

19
NOVEMBER

Knock, knock!
Who's there?
Cynthia.
Cynthia who?
Cynthia been away, I've missed you.

20
NOVEMBER

Knock, knock!
Who's there?
Manny.
Manny who?
Manny people keep asking me that!

21
NOVEMBER

Knock, knock!
Who's there?
Desdemona.
Desdemona who?
Desdemona Lisa always have a smile on her face?
(try an Italian accent)

22
NOVEMBER

Knock, knock!
Who's there?
Eisenhower.
Eisenhower who?
Eisenhower late for work this morning.

23
NOVEMBER

Knock, knock!
Who's there?
Evita.
Evita who?
Evita been ready we wouldn't be late.

24
NOVEMBER

Knock, knock!
Who's there?
Ewan.
Ewan who?
You and me are supposed to be going out tonight.

25
NOVEMBER

Knock, knock!
Who's there?
Heidi.
Heidi who?
No, it's hi-dee-ho.

26

NOVEMBER

Knock, knock!
Who's there?
Mabel!
Mabel who?
Mabel doesn't work either!

27

NOVEMBER

Knock, knock!
Who's there?
Hugo.
Hugo who?
Hugo your way, I'll go mine.

28

NOVEMBER

Knock, knock!
Who's there?
Ivan
Ivan who?
Ivan to be alone.

29
NOVEMBER

Knock, knock!
Who's there?
Jess.
Jess who?
Jess me!

30
NOVEMBER

Knock, knock!
Who's there?
Judah.
Judah who?
Judah man!

DECEMBER

Knock, knock!
Who's there?
Avery.
Avery who?
Avery merry Christmas to you!

1

DECEMBER

Knock, knock!
Who's there?
Honda.
Honda who?
Hon-da first day of Christmas, my true love gave to me.

2

DECEMBER

Knock, knock!
Who's there?
Brittney Spears.
Brittney Spears who?
Knock, knock!
Who's there?
Oops! I did it again!

3

DECEMBER

Knock, knock!
Who's there?
Barry.
Barry who?
Barry nice to see you!

4

DECEMBER

Knock, knock!
Who's there?
Bean.
Bean who?
Bean a while since I last saw you!

5

DECEMBER

Knock, knock!
Who's there?
Esther.
Esther who?
Esther anything I can do for you?

6
DECEMBER

Knock, knock!
Who's there?
Linda.
Linda who?
Linda hand, I can't be expected to do it all by myself!

7
DECEMBER

Knock, knock!
Who's there?
Jess.
Jess who?
Jess me telling you a knock-knock joke.

8
DECEMBER

Knock, knock!
Who's there?
Wet.
Wet who?
Wet me in, it's waining out here!

9

DECEMBER

Knock, knock!
Who's there?
Adam.
Adam who?
Adam if I do, and Adam if I don't.

10

DECEMBER

Knock, knock.
Who's there?
Yule.
Yule who?
Yule never know!

11

DECEMBER

Knock, knock!
Who's there?
Police.
Police who?
Police hurry up, it's chilly outside!

12

DECEMBER

Knock knock.
Who's there?
Shirley!
Shirley who?
Shirley you must know me by now!

13

DECEMBER

Knock knock.
Who's there?
Keanu.
Keanu who?
Keanu let me in, it's cold out here!

14
DECEMBER

Knock knock.
Who's there?
Ho, ho.
Ho, ho who?
You know, your Santa impression could use a little work.

15
DECEMBER

Knock, knock!
Who's there?
Fozzie.
Fozzie who?
Fozzie hundredth time, let me in!

16
DECEMBER

Knock, knock!
Who's there?
Justice!
Justice who!
Justice as I thought, you don't remember me!

17

DECEMBER

Knock, knock!
Who's there?
Kent.
Kent who?
Kent you tell who it is?

18

DECEMBER

Knock, knock!
Who's there?
Lenin.
Lenin who?
Lenin too far back in your chair is dangerous.
You might fall over.

19

DECEMBER

Knock, knock!
Who's there?
Lionel.
Lionel who?
Lionel get you nowhere.
(said in an Irish accent)

20

DECEMBER

Knock, knock!
Who's there?
Mandy.
Mandy who?
Mandy lifeboats, we're sinking!

21
DECEMBER

Knock, knock!
Who's there?
Matthew!
Matthew who?
Mat-thew lace has come undone, can you tie it?

22
DECEMBER

Knock, knock!
Who's there?
Olive.
Olive who?
Olive across the road.

23
DECEMBER

Knock, knock!
Who's there?
Omar.
Omar who?
Omar goodness! I'm locked out.

24
DECEMBER

Knock, knock!
Who's there?
Paul.
Paul who?
Paul up a chair and I'll tell you!

25
DECEMBER

Knock, knock.
Who's there?
Irish.
Irish who?
Irish you a Merry Christmas!

26
DECEMBER

Knock, knock.
Who's there?
Mary.
Mary who?
Mary Christmas!

27
DECEMBER

Knock, knock!
Who's there?
Darby.
Darby who?
Dar-by a lot of reasons why I knocked.

28
DECEMBER

Knock, knock!
Who's there?
Juan.
Juan who?
Juan to hear any more knock-knock jokes?

29
DECEMBER

Knock, knock!
Who's there?
Fanny.
Fanny who?
Fanny the way you keep saying 'Who's there' every time I knock!

30

DECEMBER

Knock, knock!
Who's there?
Knee.
Knee who?
Knee-d you ask?

31

DECEMBER

Knock, knock!

Who's there?

Celeste.

Celeste who?

Celeste time I'm going to tell this joke!

CONCLUSION

Knock, knock!
Who's there?
Toodle.
Toodle who?
Bye, bye!

We hope you've learned a great deal about the Knock-Knock joke; how to deliver one perfectly, and enjoyed going through our collection.

Now that you have the knowledge, the skills, and 366 jokes to get through, it's time to get started on your beloved victims! You'll be promoted from 'Dad' to 'Fun Dad' in no time!

If you enjoyed this book, please leave a review on Amazon. Also, if you have a favorite Knock Knock joke, remember to include it! We love to read them.

OUR GIFT

TWO SPECIAL GIFTS FOR OUR READERS

AS A SPECIAL THANK YOU FOR GETTING THIS BOOK, WE'D LIKE TO GIVE YOU:

A BOOK EXCLUSIVE (AVAILABLE ONLY WITH THIS BOOK)

THE SURPRISING PSYCHOLOGY OF LAUGHTER, AND 10 UNIQUE TOOLS & TECHNIQUES FOR YOU TO MAKE LAUGHTER AN EVERYDAY HABIT FOR THE FAMILY

+

New Message

To: theluckyreader@message.com

Subject: Dad Joke of the Day!

WHY DID THE GOLFER CHANGE HIS PANTS?

BECAUSE HE GOT A HOLE IN ONE!

A MONTH OF FRESH DAD JOKES

IF YOU LIKE KNOCK KNOCK JOKES, THEN HERE'S AN EXTRA 31 DAYS OF FRESH DAD JOKES TO USE ON YOUR UNSUSPECTING VICTIM!

VISIT WWW.DADDILIFE.COM/LOL TO GET YOURS!

REFERENCES

Knock, knock!
Who's there?
Tickle.
Tickle who?
Tickle look at these sites!

FURTHER READING

1. https://www.npr.org/sections/npr-history-dept/2015/03/03/389865887/the-secret-history-of-knock-knock-jokes

2. https://www.knockknockjokes.nu

3. https://frugalfun4boys.com/knock-knock-jokes-for-kids/

4. https://parade.com/944054/parade/knock-knock-jokes/

5. https://www.rd.com/list/knock-knock-jokes-for-kids/

6. https://www.familyminded.com/s/best-knock-knock-jokes-dc9cdf3cb12c4c3e

7. https://www.ducksters.com/jokes/knockknock.php

8. https://www.goodhousekeeping.com/life/parenting/g28581033/best-jokes-for-kids/

9. https://bestlifeonline.com/knock-knock-jokes/

ACKNOWLEDGEMENTS

A massive thank you to the DaddiLife writers – especially Marc and Jon for their countless hours of inspiration and good humor in putting this book.

A very special thank you too to Emilie Dorange and Jon Shortt. Emilie in particular for her design wizardry, and Jon in particular for his absolutely amazing illustrations that we've enjoyed laughing at more than we should have!

Made in the USA
Las Vegas, NV
19 December 2021

38851905R00111